OUT OF THE STRONG, SOMETHING SWEET

GOITSEONE SEKOLOKWANE

ISBN: 978-0-692-16424-2

Printed in the United States of America by:

This book is printed on acid-free paper.

All scripture quotations are from the King James Version of the Bible, except otherwise stated.

DEDICATION

This book is for those who are facing challenges or strange situations, discouragement, and hopelessness. I want to say to you all, I have been in the midst of that burning heat of Egypt, and today, I'm out and a witness to the power of God. I know that our situations are different as Christians, and there's nothing bigger than our God Himself. Your situation might be sickness, rejection, barrenness, unemployment, loneliness, or divorce; perhaps you are in prison, or you have a court case or whatever such situation. All may seem silent, but trust me, God is aware and He is still saying something, as long as your eyes focus on the cross—where our help is coming from. My advice is, the God who sees your tears privately will wipe your eyes and open up your testimony publicly. Whatever it is that is eating you now, you are about to enjoy honey from it in Jesus' Name, Amen!

Remain focused on His word. Thank you.

ACKNOWLEDGMENTS

I give God the glory, who gave me wisdom and ability to write this book. I thank and appreciate the Prophet of God, Prophet T.B. Joshua whom the Lord used for healing and delivering my daughter.

To my lovely husband, Monty Sekolokwane, I want to acknowledge you for the role you played in this book to becoming a reality. I thank my editors, designers, and publishers.
The Attorney, Brandy S. Reeves who played a role in the court case, I thank you.

Thank you Pastor Lyndsay Lee Slocum for supporting us from the beginning of the situation till today.
To all the teams of Grady Health Hospital and Children's Health Care of Atlanta at Egleston and the specialists: pulmonologists, ENT specialists, gastrointestinal specialists, cardiologists, neurologists, dieticians, speech therapists, physical therapists and the list goes...
- Remain blessed, you all -

OUT OF THE STRONG,

SOMETHING SWEET

(Judges 14: 14)

TABLE OF CONTENTS

FOREWORD

Goitseone Sekolokwane's book is a beautiful story of God at work in ways bigger than humans can ever imagine. Goitseone shares with vulnerability and honesty about her difficult journey through hardship and gives praise to God for mercy, healing and deliverance from tragedy. Anyone who reads this book will walk away with a deeper appreciation of the overwhelming sweetness of God's provision.

Thanks for sharing your book with me!

Lyndsay Lee Slocum
Senior Associate Pastor
Roswell Presbyterian Church
Direct Line: 770.649.4519

PREFACE

Why this title?

Out of The Strong, Something Sweet

In the Book of Judges 14 v 5 to the end, we see the story of a child of God—Samson, who was carrying a prophetic destiny. He encountered a lion (the strong or eater) but the Spirit of God came upon him, and he tore the lion apart with his bare hands. Eventually, when Samson returned to the place where he killed the lion the other time, he saw that a swarm of bees had created a hive in the carcass. He went ahead to tap the honey from the carcass of the lion that wanted to kill him.

The Strong or eater (The devil's attack in the form of a lion)

Allow me to illustrate this. You see, as a child of God, our problems might be because of a promotion that is about to come. The devil sensed that Samson is in the prophetic mission. The devil attacked Samson in the form of a lion, trying to kill him. Since God was aware, His presence empowered him, that's why he killed the lion with his bare hands. As we all know, naturally, it is impossible to kill a lion without a weapon.

Something Sweet (Testimony in the form of honey).

Sometimes, it is crucial to keep the stone that the devil used to hit you. I mean here, Samson didn't say, *I will never in my life pass through that place, a lion could eat me.* Instead, he remembered the place, passed there again, checked, and was surprised to see the dead lion issuing something sweet.

As for me, Goitseone, I kept the stone that hit me and used

it today to build the tower—I mean, the mess the devil has caused in my life is now a message to the people. The message of this book, will bring healing, encouragement, blessing, and have someone surrender his/her life to Christ.

Something Strong - *Sickness and court case that was about to take me to prison*

Something Sweet - *Testimony of miracle healing and freedom from threats of imprisonment*

I never thought I would be an author of this book until problems came, which propelled me to be one. The devil caused me to be his victim, but guess what, my God has turned me to encourage those who are weak to be strong, sick to be healed, hopeless prisoners to become prisoners of hope so that they will be free by faith and can also divert a sinner into the kingdom of God. **What is it that's trying to eat you?**

INTRODUCTION

Out of the Strong, Something Sweet is based on the living experience of the author, Goitseone Sekolokwane, who was inspired to write this book after passing through many trials that ended as testimonies. God proved His presence in her life even in the midst of trouble, confirming that He's still the same yesterday, today, and forever. God does visit us during our trying times so that we can know, see, recognize, and realize that, indeed, He is real. It's not enough to read such experiences only from the Bible or just see others' testimonies. The point is, how shall we taste His power? The more we experience situations, the more He appears to us so we may experience and trust Him—that's why our condition is not like others'. There's no way we can see His glory and remain silent, no matter what it is; His signs and wonders provoke us to be witness to others. The fire will be birth in us to say it even when people try to stop it, but no one can remove our encounters with God.

As it was written concerning Hannah in **1 Samuel 1:6** –

And her adversary also provoked her sore, for to make her fret, because the LORD had shut up her womb.

God knew about her situation; it didn't surprise Him. God used that avenue to draw Hannah close to Him. Whatever Satan intended for bad or evil, God meant it for good. The womb that was barren was prepared to hold a great child, Samuel, who would be a prophet that would ordain kings. The pain she suffered turned to joy. She is heaven's hero that even in our generations, we are still referring to her story, as others even console or strengthen themselves with her story.

Hope

I too; my situation today is a testimony that will be remembered by the next generation who reads my story, encouraging themselves by it to gain strength and win their battles.

You too; you will shake off your pain, knowing that something hidden is about to come from that reproach and shame or whatever situation you may be. Amen!

The Importance of Being Born Again

You may not be born again, but if you happen to be in a dire situation, know that you might as well be alone. You need God's intervention because you can't face a lion without a weapon, it will eat you. However, with God, it's possible, to experience the miraculous, like Samson did to a lion without anything in his hands except the power of God. Read on for your understanding.

John 8:32 says:- *And ye shall know the truth, and the truth shall make you free.* When understanding comes, victory follows. You need to be born again so that you can have access and security by the blood of Jesus. David said in the favorite verse of Psalms 23 that *"Yea, though I walk through the valley of the shadow of death, I will fear no evil."*

Why? Because he knew that he is protected by the power of

God.

Can you imagine becoming the devil's food just because you are not saved? This is what I adapted from one of the leading God's servants in our generation, Dr. Bishop David Oyedepo, when he said: **For those who keep poultry, the food you give to your poultry birds is not a show of love, but purely a business strategy, the more you feed the bird, the fatter it becomes, waiting for the day of slaughter.**

Now, this is exactly what Satan does to people. His attractive love has a motive behind it—to destroy at the end.

Refuse to be the devil's food by letting Jesus into your life because when you hand over the key to Him, even if you are in a dire situation, it will never be like others. This is the answer only when you're what? Born Again.

Being born again here means being born of the Spirit of God.

Read the conversation of Jesus and Nicodemus in *John 3:1-21*:

'There was a man of the Pharisees, named Nicodemus, a ruler of the Jews:

²The same came to Jesus by night, and said unto him, Rabbi, we know that thou art a teacher come from God: for no man can do these miracles that thou doest, except God be with him.

³Jesus answered and said unto him, Verily, verily, I say unto thee, Except a man be born again, he cannot see the kingdom of God.

⁴Nicodemus saith unto him, How can a man be born when he is old? can he enter the second time into his mother's womb, and be born?

⁵Jesus answered, Verily, verily, I say unto thee, Except a man be born of water and of the Spirit, he cannot enter into the kingdom of God.

⁶That which is born of the flesh is flesh; and that which is born of the Spirit is spirit.

⁷Marvel not that I said unto thee, Ye must be born again.

⁸The wind bloweth where it listeth, and thou hearest the sound thereof, but canst not tell whence it cometh, and whither it goeth: so is every one that is born of the Spirit.

9 Nicodemus answered and said unto him, How can these things be?

10 Jesus answered and said unto him, Art thou a master of Israel, and knowest not these things?

11 Verily, verily, I say unto thee, We speak that we do know, and testify that we have seen; and ye receive not our witness.

12 If I have told you earthly things, and ye believe not, how shall ye believe, if I tell you of heavenly things?

13 And no man hath ascended up to heaven, but he that came down from heaven, even the Son of man which is in heaven.

14 And as Moses lifted up the serpent in the wilderness, even so must the Son of man be lifted up:

15 That whosoever believeth in him should not perish, but have eternal life.

16 For God so loved the world, that he gave his only begotten Son, that whosoever believeth in him should not perish, but have everlasting life.

17 For God sent not his Son into the world to condemn the world; but that the world through him might be saved.

¹⁸ He that believeth on him is not condemned: but he that believeth not is condemned already, because he hath not believed in the name of the only begotten Son of God.

¹⁹ And this is the condemnation, that light is come into the world, and men loved darkness rather than light, because their deeds were evil.

²⁰ For every one that doeth evil hateth the light, neither cometh to the light, lest his deeds should be reproved.

²¹ But he that doeth truth cometh to the light, that his deeds may be made manifest, that they are wrought in God."

See now: The truth is, no one can enter the kingdom of God

unless such gets born again. When you grasp this reality, then take action, your old nature gives away, and new nature of Christ is born in you.

2 Corinthians 5:17 says, Therefore if any man be in Christ, he is a new creature: old things are passed away; behold, all things are become new. This is what I mean when I say your situation will differ, because the one who is inside of you, which is Jesus, His flesh had never been sick or even degenerated. It's true that as Christians, we can get sick, but it's for a short time. Whatever situation you find yourself in like rejection, depression, failure, barrenness or sickness, for example, are not meant to kill us. The scripture says we cannot be tempted beyond the level of our faith. You know, our God knows us better than we know ourselves.

CHAPTER ONE
MY SITUATION IS NOT LIKE OTHERS'

My Situation is Not Like Others'.

I mean, as Christians, our situations come with a hidden honey in it. Also, our problems are the announcement of promotion that is about to emerge in our lives. It is not to destroy us or harm us (**Jeremiah 29:11**); it is to prepare us for the challenges ahead. Just as it's written in the Book of Exodus when Pharaoh killed all male children that were born during the birth of Moses, you'll see that whenever God announces or releases a deliverer on this earth, Satan is already there to threaten and end that hidden promotion given to the children of God. The good thing is that Satan is always a loser; even though he killed them all, Moses escaped unscathed, and was even raised in the house of the enemy.

As for me, the mess the devil caused in my life is a message that has turned my fear to boldness. I want to share with you my personality: I was a timid person who was always hiding and didn't want to say anything because I don't like to be in the spotlight. I also like to limit myself in everything. Then guess what, the devil is no respecter of any person, and he wants us who are trying to act holy and righteous. The devil squeezed me in a way that caused me to pray in this manner and make a vow to God: *"God, rescue me from this problem, you know my great weakness is timidity. I promise you that I will shake off this shyness and put on a garment of confidence by stepping up publicly and winning souls for your kingdom."* Indeed, it came to pass; God remembered me more than my expectation. Today, I wrote this book to spread the message about His works.

The situation changed me from lamb mentality to Lion mentality (boldness).

Evidently, when God gets involved, He takes what Satan meant to destroy us and turns it to work for our good instead.

You see now that God is not cheap, and before we can boast about Him, there's always an inside story. Sometimes, we as people, wished we can be like those in the Bible, but do not consider the problems they passed through before they could gain the glory. For instance, we might wish to be like Abraham, but not all of us can withstand what he went through. There's a big challenge, but we can enjoy the great sweetness that shall emerge thereafter.

I am not a teacher, but I've experienced God in a dimension; that's why I came about this book. I am not a pastor, preacher, prophet, or whatever title you may think of, but God can use anybody, anytime, anywhere, in anything—that's why He said He could even use stones. Many of us experienced His power and had testimonies, but it depends on you and what to do with the stone that devil used to hit you.

I, Goitseone, decided to keep the stone that devil used to hit me and build a tower with it. I have never let my pain go to waste. Instead, I used it for the awareness of the kingdom of

God that rescued me. It doesn't matter whether it's small or huge, but I just chose to use it as long as God is involved. Our problems are not like others' in this world, and as a child of God, our situations are meant for good (not to shame or destroy us). God brings good out of what the enemy intended for evil.

See the Bible picture of Joseph in Genesis 50 v 20. You will realize that as Christians, our situation is not like others' indeed. We are so different; our problems cannot kill us regardless of how strong or long they may seem. What is your situation? As long as you are part of the family, you are included in the victory that Jesus claimed for us. If you are not part of the family, it's not too late and in the first chapter of this book, I explained about being born again.

CHAPTER TWO
THE BEGINNING OF EXPERIENCE IN MY SPIRITUAL LIFE

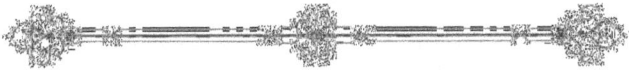

F rom my early experience, since I became a born-again Christian, my life was full of miraculous testimonies. Whenever I prayed and fasted, the miracle would manifest, and when I looked at the life of other Believers that were suffering, I would avoid them, thinking that they were not strong enough in their spiritual life. I noticed that when you are a baby Christian, God can perform big miracles for you as a sign, meaning to let you know that He is the same God who brought the children of Israel out of the bondage, from the hand of Pharaoh by performing miracles. That was how He was preparing their faith for battles ahead so that they can trust Him the more. If you read the Book of Judges where Moses and Joshua were no more among them, that's when others were even losing their lives because they had to take responsibility for moving their mountains. When you are a Christian, there are good times when you shift the mountains, and there are hard times when you must climb the mountain.

I never knew this secret until I heard from Prophet T.B. Joshua, who used to say, paraphrased **"To be a Christian doesn't mean you cannot have challenges, you can be sick as a friend of God, you can be poor, rejected, etc., but our situations are not like others but to promote us to another level, to cause us to be close to God."** I believe, you know, if you are a real Christian who has tasted His power

20

before, there's no way you can run away from God when you are in crisis. Instead, you get closer and closer to Him.

Also, **Isaiah 43:1-3** says: **But now thus saith the Lord that created thee, O Jacob, and he that formed thee, O Israel, Fear not: for I have redeemed thee, I have called thee by thy name; thou art mine.**

² When thou passest through the waters, I will be with thee; and through the rivers, they shall not overflow thee: when thou walkest through the fire, thou shalt not be burned; neither shall the flame kindle upon thee.

³ For I am the Lord thy God, the Holy One of Israel, thy Savior: I gave Egypt for thy ransom, Ethiopia and Seba for thee.

THE BEGINNING OF EXPERIENCE
IN MY SPIRITUAL LIFE

As you can see, this scripture is straight, confirming that as a Christian, we will encounter serpents and scorpions, but the good news is, we won't be destroyed. Meaning that even if we get sick, poor, rejected, etc., all these things will only strengthen our faith, drawing us closer to God. If you read it well, it's not saying if or maybe, there's an assurance here that it's a must. Now, know that our problem does not surprise God, He is aware of your situation.

I never knew that it doesn't matter how strong you are in prayers or how anointed you are, you can still encounter problems. That's why our Lord Jesus Christ prayed for us in **Luke 22:32,** *"But I have prayed for you, Simon, that your faith will not fail. And when you have turned back, strengthen your brothers."* He knew that I would face challenges regardless.

CHAPTER THREE
MY RELOCATION TO THE U.S.A.

Challenges

Things started happening after we relocated from Botswana to the United States of America on November 2010; strange things like sickness, lack of jobs, court cases, etc. I had an assurance that when I pressed on and prayed, I would get a quick answer. So, at that time, I was not even believing in any prophet yet because I knew that I had been given power and ability too to move every satanic mountain, which is true in the light of what is written in the scriptures. Not knowing that even though we have been given the power, we sometimes encounter the problems that are too strong for us, and that's why God sent prophets to us as instruments with a higher anointing to help us.

Remember, it's written in **James 5:14***: Is anyone among you sick? "He shoul♦ call in the church el♦ers* (the spiritual guides). *An♦ they shoul♦ pray for him, anointing him with oil in the Lor♦'s name."* I tried everything I could by pressing, praising, fasting, and praying all kinds of prayers until I caught the revelation one day through the teachings of a man of God, Prophet T.B Joshua, who confirmed that a Christian can have challenges but yet be a good friend of God, and immediately, hope thundered on my spirit. I gained the strength I had been missing since I had been questioning God and condemning myself that I may have done an unpardonable sin somehow, and that's why my problems were overwhelming me. When the man of God was still preaching, I also remembered the other scripture that was confirming what he said, see **Isaiah 43:2-3***: When thou passest through the waters, I will be with thee; an♦ through the rivers, they* *shall not overflow thee: when thou walkest through the fire, thou shalt*

not be burned; neither shall the flame kindle upon thee.

[3] For I am the Lord thy God, the Holy One of Israel, thy Saviour:

I gave Egypt for thy ransom, Ethiopia and Seba for thee.

Behold, I chewed it and swallowed it till I gained more

strength, and I then started slowly enjoying my test with an

understanding because, according to what I got, the scripture

is assuring us that the problems will come to us, but we will not

be consumed as I explained above.

Strength from scriptures - Living picture

The other scripture that proves this is in **1 Corinthians**

10:13 - *There hath no temptation taken you but such as is common to*

man: but God is faithful, who will not suffer you to be tempted above

that ye are able; but will with the temptation also make a way to

escape, that ye may be able to bear it. As children of destiny, our

situation is not like others indeed. You can see that most

successful people, if you ask them where they are coming from

in relation to where they are, you will notice that for gold to be

gold, it must be tested by passing through the fire to prove if it's real. You can see even the giants of faith in the bible; they were tested. There's no honey without the Eater.

There's one of the testimonies that encourages me a lot, especially when I'm in dire situations. There's a woman of God called Joyce Meyer from Missouri, USA, who went through the turmoil of abuse while growing up, according to her, and then was diagnosed with cancer later on. The Lord set her free, the cancer disappeared, and now she's over 73yrs old as I write this book and still strong, going around spreading the word of God. This is a living example of what *Our Situation is Not like others'* is like. Now, she's using her situation to win souls in the world and touching billions of people, including me. I was so inspired when I heard her living story. Many that were in her situation had their lives destroyed, some even died. Imagine if she had been killed by that cancer and abuse, these billions of people whose lives have been changed through her, where would they be? What was trying to destroy her, God meant for good; she is a vessel of God, a living witness teacher, not just teaching, an encourager and giver of hope to people like us. The abusiveness and cancer couldn't kill her. Instead, she was promoted to be what we see now. The honey she's enjoying from the Strong (Eater) is now dripping to the people, even nations, continents, everybody enjoying the sweet from the abuse that was trying to destroy the woman of God—Joyce Meyer.

CHAPTER FOUR
THIS IS MY TESTIMONY

John 3 v 11-12 - We speak of what we know and we testify to what we have seen...

Now see what happened to me:

Pregnancy

We had two boys already, but the thought of having another baby was distant. I remember back home that I used to imagine and loved seeing twin girls, and I would narrate how I would dress them so elegantly! I never knew God saw my heart, though I never prayed for them.

Now, it was the beginning of the year 2011, and I became pregnant. I was restless, developed a habit of getting nightmares, and visited the doctor continuously until the pregnancy was four months. The sickness got so bad that I ended up giving birth at an early stage of 24 weeks!

The gynecologist started bringing machines to scan my pregnancy. Alas! It revealed I was carrying twin baby girls!! This was shocking as we never thought we would be having twins, and now the thoughts of, "Why should they be twin girls, and then have issues?"

Difficult decisions – only if God is backing you

The doctors declared to me that since my babies were 24 weeks, there was no chance that they could survive because they were at an extremely premature stage and that if we decided to keep them, they wouldn't be normal at all. I inquired further, and they said, "We mean they won't be able to walk, talk, or even eat, and we will be inserting feeding tubes that they'll be using forever, so this is going to be a burden to you." I remember there was one doctor who pitied us and said, "*Why on't you release them to let them go, just to ie naturally because even if we coul try, they woul be a buren to you guys, as young as you are.*" My husband and I looked into each other's eyes, wondering if this made sense, but something thundered in my heart, and I said *No.* The next option they were looking at was to do a C-section just to save me and then let the babies die naturally, because I also had a complicated delivery. It was a very tough decision for us since that was my first time having difficulty in delivery. My husband asked them if they would survive as they did the procedure. One of the doctors replied, "*There's no guarantee of survival.*" Then my husband reasoned that it didn't make sense for me to have a procedure and at the same time, no guarantee of the babies' survival. My husband disagreed with the doctor's option. The doctors left us but uncomfortably.

In the ICU Room

Later, they transferred me to ICU, and I awaited delivery there. I spent three days without food and water, since I was on drugs, steroids, and machines. Since we rejected the doctor's option of performing a procedure, our choice was trusting God the babies would come out naturally even though it wouldn't change the fact that they would be premature. We kept on praying day and night. Since I was alone in ICU, they didn't allow anyone to enter, apart from my husband, who was permitted in once a day. He left me with a laptop to watch and pray along with the man of God, Prophet TB Joshua. I was on the bed without any movement; they inserted tubes to help me pee. I remembered shouting when the pain was critical on my back, and they gave me the drugs that they said were the strongest ones for extreme pains. I remember my heart was so bold, believing that as the Lord lives, I wouldn't die a premature death. I was singing a song with Emmanuel TV singers saying, *Lord, I believe, I believe*!!!! Later on, on the third day, God released me.

Delivery

One of the babies was in breech position; this complicated the delivery again, and they said she might strangle the other baby and make the delivery even more difficult. The doctors did not allow the bag to break as they said that was the only safe way to make them come out. The babies came out in their bag, just like a chicken laying an egg.

I delivered naturally but still premature at 24 weeks, and the doctors broke the bag and separated the babies and put them in incubators with full life support. The babies were so small that one could fit in my palm.

Later on, after about three months, one of the twins passed on because of their size.

What do you expect for a 24-week-old baby? More challenges came. I remember the doctors describing the remaining baby as the most critical premature in the hospital at that time.

At this stage, two things were possible:

1. The baby could die.

2. To live was to remain disabled for its entire life, meaning physically and mentally.

Part of the reason I wrote this book was because I have seen the healing hand of God upon my daughter. I am a witness, and it's tough to those who don't believe in the supernatural. To those who believe in the Spirit of God, they know what I am talking about, because God is a Spirit and spiritual things are understood by spiritual beings, meaning it's a mystery. That's why the Bible specified in **Mark 16:17** that - *Ant these signs shall follow them that believe; In my name shall they cast out tevils; they shall speak with new tongues;*

Life Support

I like the doctors who supported me throughout my stay; they did their job beautifully even though it was very tough, especially when they said they would need to do heart surgery (PDA), due to a hole in her heart and one of the arteries that had not closed yet, because she was still developing and, that was hindering her from getting enough oxygen to the blood. Can you imagine when the heart is not functioning, nothing can work, even when they tried to employ an oxygen machine, it was failing. I remember when the doctor pictured for us the way the lungs looked like by that time, he said; *"They look like jelly since she was under developed, very sensitive."* Glory be to God, the surgery went well, then they put her in a ventilator, inserted oxygen and feeding tubes because of severe respiratory or cardiac problems that were causing the lack of sucking and swallowing. The respiratory system and feeding system used the same passageway, causing her to aspirate, which is dangerous.

After five months, my husband and I had the classes for seven days of how to take care of our baby, since she was literally surrounded by machines. For instance, things like how to reinsert a feeding tube, in case the baby removed it while scratching herself, because no doctor would be available to stay with you in your house and assist with everyday challenges. After we passed all the classes, they released her to go home with the same situation. For a year and a half, the baby was using a feeding tube, oxygen, apnea monitor, Ox machine—all these for 24/7. Can you imagine that we were immigrants looking for green pastures in the USA, and unfortunately, we got bound by this situation?

My husband would go to a part-time job, and I had to watch our daughter 24/7, wasted time and money. This was the work of the devil just to devastate us. Huh!!! Now, it was my turn to do all I could as a Christian—praying, fasting, meditating, and praising. I even examined myself and asked God: "Where did I go wrong?" Like I said about this scripture (**Isaiah 43: 1-3**)

I caught it and my eyes open, I trusted God the more.

The Feeding Tubes

I had to make some measurements; then I would put the feeding tube through the nose, passing into the esophagus to the stomach, then I had to put the scope to listen if I inserted it well because sometimes, it could go to the lungs, and chances of catching pneumonia was very high if milk or water entered. The doctors had taught me how to differentiate the sound of when the tube was in the stomach to when it was in the lungs. Other stuff was better to deal with, like oxygen, apnea monitor, e.g., After all these thoughts and decisions, I ended up breaking the doctor's orders. I didn't know that I was putting more coal in the fire.

Nightmare - The Devil's' Trap

During this healing process, six months after the baby came home, I had a dream that my baby's pediatrician was fighting with me, and then a law enforcement officer came and arrested me. I ignored this dream (this is a spiritual fight!). The same week, I just started thinking more about the severity of using a feeding tube for more than a year; I started to lose my patience by developing fear inside of me that the tube had been in her too long, and I was thinking it could be damaging her forever and that she may forget how to feed through the mouth. I felt a pushing decision; it was strongly urging me to feed the baby by mouth. You may think nurses and doctors had always surrounded me. That was not the case, I was the one inserting the tube, and there was a high risk that it might sometimes be misplaced and life-threatening. My daughter was irritated that she would pull out the tube several times and I would keep on inserting it back. This was one of the things I hated the most and sometimes, I would cry because I was feeling for her.

Court Case Issue Started

Behold, another problem popped up. One day, the nurse visited me and noticed that I was feeding the baby by mouth, then she reported the matter to the baby's pediatrician.

This is another issue now (and remember the dream). Instead of rebuking it, I ignored it. Then the same doctor I saw in the dream sent Department of Child Services (DFCTS) personnel to my house to assess the situation. They came at an appointed time, and there were no issues according to them. Days later, the baby was booked for check-up, not knowing that would be the time of separation from my baby girl. I get overwhelmed whenever I write this part.

I can picture that meeting where there were doctors, and

DFCTS people surrounding us and announcing to us that they were retaining the baby, and we had to leave the baby and go home until we would meet at court! I was heavily sobbing, rolling in front of them, but there wasn't mercy at all. Maybe God was hardening their hearts; I don't know. This is the most painful thing I've ever felt in my life, and I was dead inside of me, only my husband was the strong one dealing with this case.

Lesson: What I Learnt and Noticed

Many people don't understand that as Christians, sometimes we encounter some problems that will associate you with irresponsible people as if you are one of them whereas Satan attacked you purposely to put you in shame, and reproach. Some Christians even find themselves in some problems and places like prisons.

In that situation, people would start thinking twice about you, not knowing that you are in bondage. For instance: The reason the people of Israel were not released by sending military to fight Pharaoh was because they were caged-in spiritually, which needed God's intervention to deliver them.

He sent one person, instead of a group of men with weapons to fight. Moses was empowered spiritually to face Pharaoh. This is what I passed through; I experienced the bondage, and I know what I'm talking about. It might be awkward to others, but the point is, you can't understand if you have not seen or experienced it. I have seen it and felt it. My situation was a shame to some because what was going through their minds was that I was irresponsible to derail from the doctor's instructions. But with God by my side, I had to go through that in order to have this message as I wrote this book.

I remember one of the chaplains at the hospital telling me that if God loves me, why would He allow me to pass through what I was going through, and why doesn't He take me out of the situation.

God uses foolish things to gain His glory. He used Pharaoh to raise Moses for him; see how the devil is stupid and blind that he didn't know he was raising the vessel of God to overcome him tomorrow. God knew before Moses was born, and even what he would pass through.

Five months fighting for the baby, I cried until I learned how to look up to God without begging for the help of any man. I matured and gained boldness. Then God appeared to me by showing me how I could get the baby. I never forgot that encounter or visitation I had with God. Oh My God! You don't know what I feel again when I'm writing this part.

God's Revelations – An Escape Route

I had a dream that I was in the big house alone and a man came to me and asked, "*Ma*＊*am, your house is very ＊irty, try to clean it as a prophet will be visiting you.*" **And I asked**, "*Which prophet?*" He replied, "*Go out, an＊ you will see him.*" Then I did.

Behold, I saw a black man with an afro. When I looked at his face, I recognized the face of a man of God, one of the great prophets of our times, Prophet T.B. Joshua of the Synagogue Church of All Nations in Nigeria – The SCOAN.

Then I woke up from the sleep. I narrated this revelation to my husband, then he said, "You got to go meet him." Indeed, my lovely husband processed the visa and flight ticket for me; I flew to Nigeria to the SCOAN to meet the prophet. You know, sometimes, we need upper anointing. I had tried with my level of faith and could not deliver myself from the dungeon I was in.

I arrived at Synagogue Church of All Nations in the middle of the week, ready to pray and meet the man of God. On Sunday at the church, I felt like I was the only one who had a huge problem. Later, during the church service, as the Prophet was preaching, my eyes were glued on him, and inside my heart, I was like if this man is from God indeed, with this kind of problem that I have, he must locate me, especially when I came here by the invitation of the Holy Spirit. Later on, it was time for the prophet to administer deliverance, healing, and prophesy. Many people received theirs, but I didn't. He didn't even come close to me. During the night, I couldn't sleep at all, and it was my last day, as I was to fly back to Atlanta USA later that afternoon.

The Deliverance

Revelation Comes Into Action

Now, the picture I saw in the revelation was now acting out physically: It was Monday afternoon, the evangelists took all the visitors to the other area called Prayer Mountain, and I was left alone in the cafeteria because I was supposed to go to the airport at around 5 pm. I sat alone sobbing in the cafeteria. Suddenly, I heard the voice of a man (one of the visitors) asking me, **"Why are you crying, madam?"** I said I needed to see the prophet, but I failed, and he said, **"Go out, the prophet is standing outside."** Behold, once I stepped outside, I saw the prophet and he looked at me with that kind of a look like, **"Are you the one?"** Both of us were communicating with our eyes like, you know when you are looking at each other but you are not sure if it's him, you know that reaction right? I know prophet knows what he was doing, but for me, it was confusion. Then I opened my mouth and said, **"Man of God, I want to see you."**

Quickly, he asked the evangelist to take me to his office. I didn't finish telling my story; the prophet was leading me as if he knew everything. Yes, he knew because he is a prophet. Then he said something that I never forget, **"Don't worry, it's well, the baby is coming back to you soon,"** and that wasn't all. **"She will be well, God will restore her."** Immediately, I

keyed into his words, and I believed it.

Something Left me

Some heaviness that was on me left immediately!
Remember, prophets are the mouthpiece of God, meaning
God's agenda or program are announced through the words of
the prophet.

Now, back to my dream, God knew how He was going to
use the prophet to locate me, but because of my ignorance and
lack of faith, I was crying, thinking it was over instead of
meditating and believing in what God showed me. I hope you
can discern why our problems get prolonged more than usual?
It's because we concentrate on what we see physically,
forgetting that God will answer us spiritually first, and then
comes physical confirmation. If I can tell you my secret; when
I look at the time, I became so hopeless, but when God say *yes*,
nobody can say *no*. It was God's time to release me from all this
shame. God's time is the best time indeed.

After this meeting, I automatically felt so light and peaceful. That heaviness went away and immediately, I went to the airport a praising woman.

Back in the USA

After I got home, I went straight to my emails. I got an email from my sister in Botswana who said that she dreamt and saw the Child Department people dropping off the child and saying, "We are so sorry." My friend too had a dream that she saw the baby looking fresh and healthy without the need for any machine. My son said he dreamed that the baby was able to walk and was running all over the house; my husband also told me that he saw the baby back home sitting on our bed. All these dreams happened after meeting the prophet and hearing his declaration. According to my belief, all these dreams were just signs that it was done in the realm of spirit and was about to manifest physically.

That same week, my husband received a call from the attorney that was involved in the hearing and the judge decided to finalize our case as soon as possible, so we had to show up.

Since they had taken away my daughter, I had two hearings, and they were always postponing the case until God gave me a way to go and see this man of God. When God is involved in a situation, it doesn't matter who's in, when the light appears, darkness flees.

God Doesn't Need Help!

I remember when I started calling all my friends who were also my witnesses to inform them the case had started. They all gave excuses, others were no longer interested, while some did not pick my calls at all!

Can you imagine at the time that I thought things were now okay because I met the man of God? Do you know why they were rejecting me? God doesn't need the help nor the strength of any man when He's fighting for you.

When you read about Gideon in **Judges 7:1-22** when he defeated the Midianites; according to Gideon as a person, he knew that when going for war, he needed a big army to fight. But God said no, I don't need men to boast and say we did it.

God asked Gideon to reduce the number of men from twenty-two thousand to ten thousand, then to three hundred—the number that they used to defeat the enemy.

You see how God works; He didn't want the self-praise of my friends to say we helped her win the case by our strong witnessing. He just wanted my husband and me, so He could deliver our enemies into our hands.

Who's on Your Side? Man Cannot Be Trusted

Back to my story. There was this other lady (our landlord where we lived) who was always on our side. I called to tell her that we had to return to court. She explained to me and said, *"Look, I am American, and I am an old woman. The way I see your case, it's very tough, especially now that you are fighting with people who're already in the system like doctors, social workers, nurses, children's department—"* (they were fifteen in number, witnessing against me) *"—you are just alone with your husband, even your friends have now run away; I am sorry to say you are going to lose this case."*

Now, I was like a prisoner of hope, but not like before. You know it hurts when people reject you, but I was very bold at that time because I met a man of God who gave me a word of prophecy that released deliverance and baptized me with strength.

I replied to the woman boldly and confidently; I asked her: *"I'm sorry, do you believe in God? Have you ever come across the story of David and Goliath in the scriptures?"*
I continued: *"I don't care how many they are in number and how loud their voices are, whether they are in the system or not, but what I need is my baby, and enough is enough."*

Remember, 1 **Samuel 17** talks about when David overcame Goliath with the sword of the word. Goliath was known to be great in battle, and he had all kinds of weapons.

Then she replied: *"Okay, we shall see then."* Indeed, that same week the court case started, and when we met our attorney, she was amazed to see my husband and me being very strong and confident and vowing the word that today, we were going back home with our baby.

Have you ever seen someone who's very clear that she's taking sides in your favor, and she's ready to do something? The judge was like that, and she didn't allow anyone talk till at the end.

She said in anger "*I ⸱on't care what the situation, to⸱ay, I am releasing the chil⸱ to the mother an⸱ I want all equipment to be ⸱roppe⸱ off at their home.*" It was so shocking to them, but for us, we knew that God was in control, because like I said, when God is involved, it doesn't matter who's on the other side of the table.

To be precise, the baby came home with all the equipment surrounding her like before, nothing was changed, and she even had a scheduled appointment for the procedure on the gullet.

The court case ended, and God didn't deny us, and He fulfilled His promises because God is not a man that He should lie.

Homecoming

Indeed, the baby came back to where she belonged, like baby Moses who grew up in the hands of the enemies at Pharaoh's palace until he became a man and realized that he didn't belong to them.

He said, *"I will rather suffer with the children of God than to enjoy the pleasure of sin." (**Hebrews 11 v 25**).*

This also reminds me of an illustration that Bishop David Oyedepo gave: **That there was a small lion that grew up with the sheep and doing everything the lambs were doing, playing around and eating grass. So, when they went to drink water at the river, lions would chase them. Then one day, when they went to drink water again, the young lion saw its image in the water and realized that it didn't look like the sheep. It remembered that it looked like the animals that used to chase them, so next time the lions came, it didn't run away as usual. So, the young lion crossed over to the lions and started behaving like a lion.**

Finally, my baby was with her own biological family, and as

you know, as genuine Christians, you cannot be comfortable with your child surrounded by machines just like that. We believe that our God can change anything because He's a repairer and He never starts what He cannot finish. Then we began to fight sickness by reminding God what His Prophet declared to the baby, that it is written that the Prophets are the mouthpiece of God (remember, Prophet T.B Joshua said: *the baby will not only come home, but she will be healed*). Soon, we started seeing movements like crawling for the first time since birth. Can you imagine at the age of 1 year? We knew that God was in control, the same month God appeared to me again with a Divine solution; to switch the doctors, because I was working with the same group of doctors that handed me to children's department.

When I'm talking about a group of doctors, I mean specialists like:

GI - takes care of eating/digestive systems and recommending food for her.

Pulmonologist - takes care of the respiratory system and Oxygen equipment.

ENT - takes care of Ear, Nose and Throat system

Ophthalmologist- for eyes

Cardiologist - the heart specialist

Therapists - both speech and physical therapists and her pediatrician who was taking care in general.

I had to make a follow-up to all, and remember the situation was for life.

This is how God appeared to me: I was sleeping when I saw a group of doctors putting on white gowns. The other one was carrying a file and told me the baby was normal; I just woke up with a loud voice in my ears that she was normal. Then I grabbed my laptop and emailed one of my good friends who is a Presbyterian Church pastor, Pastor Lyndsay, to ask her if she could take me to her kid's Pediatrician. Immediately, she scheduled an appointment with her Pediatric Physicians PC and another group of specialist doctors.

What I experienced is, you can never hear from God and remain the same. My first appointment to this new specialist was a pulmonologist (lung/breathing-related specialist).

God Uses Anything

Now, See How God Was Using This Doctor

I was in the waiting room with my baby surrounded by all sorts of machines, and they were so annoying with their incessant beeping noises. The doctor came with a lovely anger and asked: *"What's going on here? there's a lot of noise."* I tried to explain, and she said with anger, *"Remove all those machines. How old she?"* I said: *"a year and three months"*. She replied: *"Is she crawling?"* I said, *"Little and she's always on the machines 24/7. It's the doctor's order."* She asked: *"How can she crawl while you hold her with machines, are you working?"* I replied: *"No, how can I work when I have to watch her 24/7?"* Then she said: *"Great; I want to see her crawling, never put machines on her unless it's night time when you can't watch her. Just keep observing and update me; then after two weeks, come back."*

Usually, doctors don't just make changes without examinations, according to the past doctors, but this one was different, like trusting the baby can make it without machines. So, I knew that deliverance was taking place, so I didn't even care about her anger. In my heart, I said *wow*! This is the influence of the Holy Spirit.

People of God, indeed, God can use anything and anyone to fulfill His promise. This doctor was in the kind of pressure that I have never seen before. After two weeks, I went back to her, and she said: "*Now, I am going to send you to another specialist with a letter*". You know, when God intervenes, it will be like a dream. She gave me the letter written to a GI specialist, recommending him to start applying food and stop milk since the baby was more than a year and that an ENT specialist remove the feeding tube so that she can start eating normally by mouth. Indeed, they obeyed the pulmonologist recommendation. Mmmmh!!! I will never forget that day, and even now, I still have the letter with me; I filed it. My baby started eating well by mouth. Now, seeing her, I am talking about the baby who failed swallow study six times and was already booked for surgery to put the tube in her belly forever, a recommendation from the first doctors. Whenever light appears, darkness flees; this is God because He's the creator. He also has the power to destroy and also repair what is broken. He can do anything. The doctors treat but God heals, and His healing is permanent. Hallelujah!

Brethren, our God is still doing miracles even now. My baby never went back to machines again and within five months; she did everything the normal way like other babies who were born at their full term. Those who have seen this kind of prematurity, I'm talking about (24 weeks) know it's the most premature a baby could be; I could hold them in my palm. There is no assurance that babies this premature could survive because it's abnormal, and unless God can intervene like He did with my daughter, they might not survive. You know some people limit God, saying there are things He can't change, but I don't care because I have seen with my own eyes what He can do and no one can take it away from me. I am talking about the baby who weighed 0.6lbs—not even a pound. Can you imagine? I remember my husband taking a video at the hospital by demonstrating how tiny she was.

He removed his wedding ring and slid it on my baby's arm, not baby's finger but arm, and it was loose, now you can imagine how small a 24-week-old baby is!

Then, after six months, we went to visit the doctor who was under the pressure of quick recovery for my baby whom I believed was under the influence of Holy Spirit; she was calm. Mmm-mm! She called me and said she noticed that I didn't take the baby to the test. *"Can you please call Scottish Rite Hospital and schedule an appointment for sleeping study and swallow study for her?",* she asked. Usually, this is what she was supposed to have done before removing the machines, but what's amazing is that she hijacked the process by removing all the machines without even checking. That's why I said she was under the influence of the Holy Spirit. Like I said before that when God interferes, it's going to be like a dream, doctor's orders don't work. Jesus is a healing balm; He's a great divine practitioner. I did what the doctor ordered me to; I scheduled an appointment for all tests where she did very well. All surgeries that were booked were canceled, then we stopped therapy appointments too because she was already eating by mouth very well, even physical activities like walking and talking, she passed all of them. Today, I am talking about a child who is no longer on medications.

You know people; it's too hard for them to believe as one day, I met a lady whose child had a similar situation like mine. She was gossiping, and this is what she said: *"This lady is a pathological liar when she said her baby is free, but I know that during the night, they could be supporting her with the machine because I too do that to my child the rest of her life."* I want to illustrate on what she said, that her doubting was not wrong according to her because she knows the seriousness of this kind of situation since her daughter is like that and for them, it's for life because her daughter is 18 years old now, and still needs the support of machines. The point is even if we are in the same situations, when you carry God, your case is not forever, and neither can it destroy you. Remember, carnal people will never understand the things of Spirit no matter what you do until they become part of us. We spiritual Christians believe that there's nothing too big for our God to handle. We believe that

He's still the same yesterday, today and forever. We also believe in miracles, and they're working for us. **John 3:11** says "**Verily, verily, I say unto thee, we speak that we do know, and testify that we have seen; and ye receive not our witness.**" Even the scripture confirms this doubt, so there's nothing we can do about it unless God can appear to you, then you will feel what I'm feeling even when I'm writing this. I can feel His presence, reminding me that time of His visitation when I was in that situation. I want to tell you that my daughter is five years and she has never been hospitalized or had any sickness except fever like other kids at cold times. I want to further address the point of that lady, to say even at night, we don't apply anything or support her with any machine. She is completely healed. *My husband always says she's transformed, because she was not fully formed in the first place.*

The Situation Before deliverance and After

Now, in this testimony, you will notice that there's a lot of differences before I received deliverance and after. Before deliverance, there was a lot of rejection, hatred, pain, sickness, bondage and I was encountering nightmares all the time. Satan is very tricky when he attacks; he uses something that will sound reasonable to the people. For spiritually discerning person can understand, especially one who has had such experience before because the things of God are mysterious. That's why the Bible says in **1 Corinthians 2:14** that, *But the natural man receiveth not the things of the Spirit of God: for they are foolishness unto him: neither can he know them, because they are spiritually discerned.* In this stage, canal people will never understand you until deliverance takes place. Why? These things happened in the spiritual realm first then manifest in the natural. For instance; I had a dream that the police officer caught me, and I fought with the pediatrics for my baby, but I ignored all dreams because I wasn't sensitive enough in the spirit. I didn't pray against it. At the end, 2 weeks after these dreams then action took over, I started to have a thought to remove the baby's tube. Now the dream manifested in the natural when pediatrician took the issue to court.

This is what I meant; court case opened for me. You see, it sounded well to people that I disobeyed the doctors order. Do you think, anybody could care about your dreams? and you know you cannot even mention it because it was going to sound weird.

This is when you feel tormented and restless in your soul. In my case I knew that, this thing happened in the spirit and I ignored it.

Look at a very good example in this scripture of **Numbers 22 v 4** *And Moab said unto the elders of Midian, "Now shall this company lick up all that are round about us, as the ox licketh up the grass of the field." And Balak the son of Zippor was king of the Moabites at that time.*

[5] *He sent messengers therefore unto Balaam the son of Beor at Pethor, which is by the river of the land of the children of his people, to call him, saying, "Behold, there is a people come out from Egypt. Behold, they cover the face of the earth, and they abide over against me.*

⁶ Come now therefore, I pray thee, curse for me this people; for they are too mighty for me. Perhaps I shall prevail, that we may smite them, and that I may drive them out of the land; for I know that he whom thou blessest is blessed, and he whom thou cursest is cursed."

See, you are a threat to the enemies of what you will become, or you are. People are so wicked, you are buzz focused in your destiny, for them you are a threat and planning how can they destroy you. They can use anything foolish to mess you up.

You see Balak knows that, for him to be able to attack or defeat the Israelites is to curse them first, put them in confusion. He knew that even if they are many in numbers than them, it's still doesn't matter but as long as they are cursed, he will able to defeat them in the natural.

Curse means to attack in the realm of the spirit, because when you are cursed, you are in bondage, and anything foolish could happen to you in natural. For instance: maybe you are working, no promotion, whatever you lay hands on, failure, your body attracts sickness and disease, bad luck or anything you may call problem.

When you go to my court case. I told you that I saw it in the dream before appearing in the natural, right?. Why dream? When a curse happened in the spirit, God alarmed me through the dream because He is spirit and sees things of spirit and a dream is the one of ways God communicates to us the most. It is only that I was blind and ignored it.

If you are reading this part and you are in a situation that you did something wrong but you are crying and you don't know how and why you did that. Like your divorce, you feel suicide, you quit job in anger, you drop off from school or anything that would make you feel confused at the end. My friend you are under attack and you really need deliverance, because in this case only God can rescue you.

After deliverance was over

Well, darkness and light don't go together. This is when even carnal people could now listen to you and understand you. When I go back to Numbers 22, these people already were under the umbrella of God, I mean already blessed. God knows that if they could be cursed they would be defeated. Nothing could happen in the presence of God. He saw Balak's plans and

he sent an Angel to oppose Balaam not to curse his children.

Numbers 22 v 12; *And God said unto Balaam, "Thou shalt not go*

with them. Thou shalt not curse the people, for they are blessed."

Whom the Lord blessed then who can curse? If God gave

you that position, wife, husband, business, kids, certificate,

whatever may it be, then you have the grace under God to

protect it. The enemies will hire each other to take away from

you, but they will fail because God will bring deliverance.

Based on my true story: After I met Prophet, deliverance

took place, the curse broken, my daughter got healed, Judges,

doctors and everybody started understanding me, they pitied

me and close up the court case. I remember after court case they

gave us reconciliation letter to meet our opponents. After 2

weeks we met to the office for reconciliation. When we got in

the court office, the lady met us and said *she just received the*

phone call from children's Care Department that they won't come

because they trusted us, also they noticed that we are humbled and

responsible people , they are really sorry for what happened. That was the en until now.

The Doctor too pled forgiveness and she said: *it wasn't her intension to open the case for us. She thought that when she reporte the matter, they will sen the nurse assistant to assist me because there wasn't no any harm in the baby though I broke the or er, an that the baby's examination appeare goo .*

You see the reason why you have a degree but you don't get job, no man sees you to marry? Deliverance has to take place. Shake off, begin to pray and God will direct you.

As a Christian, I knew what was going on, and there's something spiritual that needed to be fixed.

I kept on praying and pressing with the level of my faith until God remembered me. See how things changed: God aligned me with someone highly anointed and as a spiritual elder to me.

James 5:14 -15; [14] *Is any sick among you? let him call for the el ers of the church; an let them pray over him, anointing him with oil in the name of the Lor :*

[15] *An the prayer of faith shall save the sick, an the Lor shall raise him up; an if he have committe sins, they shall be forgiven him.*

After Prophet T.B. Joshua declared the word of prophecy, I grabbed it and keyed into it. That's when darkness disappeared—and heaviness of stress, then I felt so light. Thereafter I got connected with the right people; my baby got healed, and what has had her bound was loosed in a way that the new doctors even forgot to follow the process. They just removed the machines without any fear until they noticed after some months that they needed to go back to the process, but that was just a confirmation that indeed, the baby was well. Can you imagine what kind of power it is that turns things around so quickly? Also, the court case was dissolved, and the power of God brought my baby back to where she belongs. What an awesome God we serve; the storm calmed in every area of our life. It's written in the Bible that every knee must bow and every tongue must confess when we mention His name—Jesus!

CHAPTER FIVE
A PROPHET—GOD'S WEAPON

T he other thing you need to realize is the importance of having a prophet in our midst. Yes, we have been given power and authority, but the level of our faith differs. We also have what I call self-deliverance, meaning; You can be able to deliver yourself through your prayer and reading the word without hand of any man or prophet. There's a time when we face mountaintop, when God now assigns a prophet to free you. When you read the whole Book of Judges, it's all about sin and repentance, and it also shows the mercy of God that whenever they cry unto Him, He will raise a leader to deliver them. Nowadays, you will see many will rather die or suffer, saying, our Lord Jesus Christ has given us grace, and I won't go to any man like prophets. I agree we have been given grace but still, God has never stopped sending His prophets to every generation. Even in the New Testament in the **Book of Acts 21:10-33**, it talks about the prophet named Agabus, who predicted that Paul would be arrested, and it came to pass. Though in the Bible, it's written that we have to be careful because other prophets are wolves hiding inside the sheepskins. I can encourage you that when you are in situations that you tried all kinds of weapons; applied the word, praising, meditating, prayed all kinds of prayers but still nothing changed for the better, I think you need to see someone with a higher spiritual authority than you. We have cadres in the spiritual realm.

Look here; I'm a living sign of the works of God through the prophet. I received my own deliverance and healing, just immediately after Prophet T.B. Joshua declared the word but not even touching me. I know you may ask yourself like; really, just saying the word? Yes! because prophets are the mouthpiece of *Go*. See: *And he shall be thy spokesman unto the people: and he shall be, even he shall be to thee instead of a mouth, and thou shalt be to him instead of God.* whenever they declare the word for you, it's automatically creates, then manifests in natural, depending on what kind of problem you have. Prophet T.B. Joshua declared a simple word *"it is well"* without even speaking in tongues. What was amazing is, the child he declared the word to, was not even there with me. He looked at my daughter's photo and said, "it is well". In that night, those who are close to me like; my husband, son, sisters and friends had different dreams that they saw my daughter healed and free. Do you see the difference between us and a prophet? Their mouth carries the word of God. This is the same word that from the beginning has created the heaven and the earth as it is written **John 1 v1-3;** *In the beginning was the Word, and the Word was with God, and the Word was God. The same was in the beginning with God. All things were made by him; and without him was not anything made that was made.*

67

How powerful is the word of God, so creative and strong? Then what is your situation that is bigger than His word? Prophets have been given that access to speak on our behalf, if you could fail yourself. I like this scripture again that's describing the word of God in **Hebrews 4 v 12.** *For the word of*

God is quick, and powerful, and sharper than any two-edged sword, piercing even to the dividing asunder of soul and spirit, and of the joints and marrow, and is a discerner of the thoughts and intents of the heart.

My advice: One thing I like about the prophet that God used to fix our problem is; His God given anointing can reach out to you there. So I don't care what part of world you are; if you can't see him, and you are sick or whatever situation you may be; go to YouTube and look for any prayers of Prophet T.B. Joshua, pray along with him then you will receive your own testimony.

Note this; I'm not saying the other prophets are not right. I'm just saying what I know, tasted, saw and witnessed. I really value my testimony regardless how it sounds to others, but for me, that's why came up with this book.

CHAPTER SIX
YOU HAVE A ROLE TO PLAY

For your prophecy to be fulfilled, you too, you have a role to play in your faith by agreeing with God.

In **Isaiah 43v26;** it says *Put me in remembrance: let us plead together: declare thou, that thou mayest be justified.*

It means remind Me My words, don't just sit religiously waiting for the word to come to pass.

Maybe you received the word of prophecy from the Prophet doesn't mean you have to wait to see if it will come to pass, like waiting to see if He's from God. According to my past experience, prophecy could delay sometimes but you have to keep on reminding God his words, when you do that, you trigger prophecy to be fulfilled and more revelations that will assure you that He is still aware of your case.

You can also trigger prophecy to be fulfilled by praising God. To praise shows that you trust what you received even though in the natural it hasn't appeared yet. Look at Gideon in **Judges: 7v13** *and it was so, when Gideon heard the telling of the*

dream, and the interpretation thereof, that he worshipped, and returned into the host of Israel, and said, Arise; for the LORD hath delivered into your hand the host of Midian. You see! Just to hear a dream, for him was a sign that already the enemy has handed into his hand, they are defeated. Gideon started to praise God, by faith believing it is done though it was not in the physical.

When God sent Gideon, He promised that he will go with him. You see that God cannot deny himself, He always keeps His promise.

You may receive His promise through dream, catch the scripture and through the prophet. All you required is to trust like scripture the confirms; **Psalm 22 v 4;** *Our fathers trusted in* *thee: they trusted, and thou didst deliver them.*

God is quick to deliver your case when you trust him the most.

To show you a living confirmation:

When I was crying during my trial, God revealed prophet T.B. Joshua to me that, he'll deliver my case. I acted physically by going to see him because I believed my dream. After I met him then there followed multiple dreams to different people as a sign that God has done it. Like I said my daughter was sick and prophet declared the word "it is well". My friends and family saw the baby healed in the dream. My son says I saw her chasing me and looking grown up but in the physical she was still in the machines, no talking, and no eating by mouth, even not crawling. My friend dreamt her talking. When I heard this, I was full of joy, I woke-up with the songs every day because I knew that it is done, moreover I honored and trusted the prophet He sent to deliver my case.

Today it came to pass like Gideon, the dream acted in the natural, it was fulfilled.

You too keep on pressing, don't give-up. We are serving the living God.

CHAPTER SEVEN
OUR WEAKNESSES

Impatience

When we are in dire situations sometimes, we don't want to be patient. We just want to jump the gun, which is caused by fear. Most of us we delay our answers by trying to sort out things by ourselves, not waiting for God's time, but the sad news is if we dodge to face trial in an attempt to beat the gun, we will still be called to start afresh, thereby staying long on correction.

Catch-up now on this from the above testimony: Doctors gave me an order of "don't feed the baby by mouth." Guess what, with my desperate sight of my daughter dying slowly, I broke the rule to feed her by mouth. I know your question is why? Impatience, according to me as a mother, the intention was not to harm her but to save her because I knew that since birth, she had never used the esophagus and this part was almost dead. The doctor told me that if the year passed and she still used this tube, then I should forget about her being able to talk and taking food through the mouth. Now, you see how situations can control us. I was full of fear then, and I took a shortcut, not knowing that I was heaping hot coals on the matter the more.

See now that the other problem with court started on top of the baby's sickness and now the prayer had to be increased. I was concentrating on God to help with the release of the child and to be healed, then instead of the answer, the court case arose again. Maybe if I could have just waited for God to take control of the sickness, I wouldn't have been involved in court case matters because God was aware and He knew that in His own time, the baby would be free from sickness. So, the way I acted during my trial, I was trying to help God and dodge the test. Instead, I prolonged the trial time.

We focus on problems, then give birth to thoughts, then decisions lead to you acting on it, and then comes the manifestations of the results of our consequences. If you focus on good things, you will produce good fruits, but if you focus on bad stuff, you will produce bad fruits. But if you let the Spirit of God lead you, you will have good thoughts. Then you will be able to take right decisions that will conduct your action which will manifest satisfactory results. When you see successful people in life, it's not by accident or luck; it's their choice of what they focused on—thoughts, decisions, etc., that gave birth to their success.

The good thing is as believers, our situations force us to be closer to God the more the problems grow. Can you imagine in my case, a mother sleeping every day without her baby! This was the most painful experience I ever encountered in my life, but the God I serve is so merciful that He remembered me because He sees beyond our wrongs.

My Advice

As a child of God, be careful not to let your situations

control you. Instead, control it by drawing the strength from the word of God. Focus on Him by listening to the teachings of men and women of God because, when we are in situations sometimes, even if you try to read the Bible without anyone leading you, you might get confused.

For example: I was praying, reading the Bible, fasting, crying to God to solve the problem so quickly because I didn't believe in having long-term issues as a child of God, but my effort failed until I started to listen to messages from men of God. Then I caught the revelation.

The Man of God, Prophet T.B. Joshua, said: "**That you face challenges does not mean you are not a friend of God or that you find yourself between a rock and a hard place does not mean you are not a candidate of Heaven. The spiritual benefit is that we will learn to pray the more, trust God the more, depend on God the more, have faith in Him.**" I was like, really?!! I got it, then my prayer line changed. In short, my advice is, if you tried everything you could and felt like God didn't exist, ask help from anointed ministers.

I am one of the Christians who believes in the prophetic ministry. There are different people who have mixed feelings concerning prophets. We have three categories which are negative people, neutral people, and positive people. It's written in the Bible that tests all spirits…

When God Is Speaking

The other thing I experienced during my trial was ignorance when God was speaking.

God can speak in many ways, anything, anytime. In my case, I'm still learning every day, but in this testimony, I had dreams. We are not supposed to ignore dreams because they have a message all the time, either bad or good. Even though we may not understand the meaning but when God sees that you are willing to understand, He can still make a way again so that you can comprehend. It's written in the **Book of Luke 21:36** that always be on the watch, and pray that you may be able to escape all that is about to happen. Our problem is that we kept on praying, praying in a way that we will hear ourselves, God cannot hear us, to the extent that we get devastated and fall into the trap of satan at the end.

How do I know this? In my testimony, remember that I had that dream that I had an encounter with my baby's doctor, then she sent the law enforcement officers to arrest me. You see, there was an alarming message that something was not right, but I just took it for granted. The other thing I experienced during my challenges is that when you are in a relationship with God; there's no way anyhow danger can come to you without you being forewarned. Now, back to the dream. This kind of dream is bad, isn't it? But no one likes bad stuff, right? And what happened according to my experience is I failed to play my role, and I ignored it and kept on praying without even listening and watching because prayer is a spiritual conversation with our Father. You know, when you talk to someone, there's a time to pause a little bit and listen to him/her, not just talking. At this point, you will miss a lot. God is good all the time, and He hears our prayers and supplications.

When you are stubborn, you will stay in rectification until you notice your mistakes.

My Advice

Since I experienced this, I would advise you never to ignore any dream, even if you don't understand it. Instead, ask God, and He will reveal it to you. When I went through my reading the Bible, I also noticed that since Genesis, God has been speaking in dreams and even now, He still does the same to us. The point is, we don't take dreams seriously like the Bible people. Like I said, I'm not a pastor or evangelist; I just say what I know and have experienced.

CHAPTER EIGHT
DOUBT

Doubt

God doesn't mind doubt, so long as you are searching the truth. Back again to my testimony, you will notice that I doubted even when God spoke to me.

Remember the picture that was a direction from God: I was crying, then He answered me by showing me how my problem would end. This time around, I obeyed God, and I flew to Nigeria, and I spent five days there.

See when my doubt came in: During the service, I said in my heart: If this man indeed is from God, he must locate me because God cannot direct me to him and he can't say even a word to me unless the dream was not from God. The doubt here was that I was not sure whether the man of God or what I heard was really from God. Then nothing happened while others were receiving their prophecy and deliverance, etc., and like I said, I was even worse—the doubt kept on expanding in my heart especially the next day because I had to go back since that was my last day there. I couldn't believe I was going to go back the same way I came.

The good point is when God says Yes, nobody can say no. Can you imagine that the last day of the last hour was when God fulfilled His promise? What was amazing and exciting at the same time is that the spiritual picture came physically as it was shown to me in the dream. Children of God, even as I am writing now, I can see what was going on at that time, and I can feel His presence now. Whenever I explain this part, people will pause and say, wait a minute: "Are you saying you were dreaming or saw it live?" and I will reply that it is both. God showed me very clearly before I can even think to come to Synagogue Church of All Nations. This part also reminds me when Saul met prophet Samuel; it was already arranged because God revealed to His prophet that Saul will come and when he comes, he must anoint him. Let me say this to you, I doubted God, but He doesn't mind doubt, as long as you need the truth. I can call it righteous doubt because I was demanding the truth, and it came to pass. I was full of divine strength and believed in my heart, and I don't care how the situation may look; the point is, it's settled.

My faith was elevated immediately when I realized that the dream I had was manifesting physically.

I remember that on the last day with one hour to go, the prophet came down and talked to me. The question is, what caused the prophet to come down to me? This is God Himself; you see God showed me, and at the same time, He spoke to the prophet about me and how he should attend to my case. It was so amazing!

Advice

Don't condemn yourself when you doubt, especially when you are demanding the truth. God will confirm it for you. God's time is the best. Remember, I was busy concentrating on my problems and heading my way back to my country. Suddenly, He did it at the last minute. I want to say if you had an encounter with God during your trial, just leave it for Him by waiting with declarations, praising. God swore in **Isaiah 14:24:**

"The Lord of hosts hath sworn, saying, Surely as I have thought, so shall it come to pass; and as I have purposed, so shall it stand:" Just like He showed me how He would use His prophet to put an end to my problems, and it came to pass. The other advice is, sometimes, when you see a prophet attend to someone in a particular way, know that this thing has been arranged in the spiritual realm before you (according to my experience). Don't be jealous thinking that maybe the prophet is favoring him or her. No, they're just being an instrument following the order of God concerning you.

CHAPTER NINE
MIRACULOUS - FOOLISH THINGS
BECAME USEFUL

Most people kept on asking about the miraculous? We have many Christians who don't believe in the miraculous. They think it's meant for the past generations, but God is still the same today, yesterday and forever.

What's miracle? A miracle is a mystery to human beings.

This is a very good picture, for instance, in the Book of

Exodus: Can you imagine when the Israelites looked behind them, and there were enemies armed with weapons, chariots, and horses? Then they looked before them, there stood the red sea. Tell me, where would you go? Nothing but to trust in the Lord and believe in Him. But God made a way for them to pass through the sea! This is what we call a miracle. You know this kind of a miracle in the bible, is one of the incredible ones especially if you know the sea very well, that will show you that, your problem is too small to God. I grew up in a landlocked country that's surrounded by other countries, where there's no sea. I have never known how sea looked like apart from learning and see in pictures. After I relocated to the United States, then one time I visited Florida to Miami beach for vacation with the family. For me, my interest was to see the sea by my own eyes. It was so funny, when people were jubilating, moving up down half nude, I was busy trying to see how really it looks like. I remember I covered my body as if I'm not in the beach and all eyes was on me, I think looked so awkward for them and noticed that this one doesn't know the beach life, which is true indeed. My focus was on the testimony of the Israelites in the bible, I was like this is so huge! Then how did the water open for them that they got in and passed?. Another point is, you can't even see where it ends. You know I was like this God we are serving, nothing is difficult for Him.

Then what is your situation? You see that, nothing is big for God Almighty!

Now, see my picture of living miracle for today. How can 24-week-old baby recover just like that and this time around, she's living without any sort of medication. Let me illustrate again about premature of 24 weeks;

* The size was fitting on my palm

- Like I said, my husband removed his wedding ring and put on her arm, catch me very well, not her finger but the ring was still sliding on the arm.
- She was weighing…0.6lbs.
- She could not breathe on her own.
- The body couldn't produce heat by itself.

Now the question is what was the solution?

These professional doctors told me that:

There are 2 things: *To let it die natural or we will try to support but according our experience, she will be abnormal the rest of her life which you have to be prepared for that.*

You see, when those you trust them to treat, giving you this answer! Where would you go in this earth? Now back to the Israelite sea case.

It's written that: **Psalm:121 1-2;** *I will lift up mine eyes unto the hills, from whence cometh my help. My help cometh from the LORD, which made heaven and earth.*

This is the only way now, not to look to any man but unto Him where help is coming.

CHAPTER TEN
DREAMS

D reams are reality.

I experienced different dreams during this trial. I noticed and realized God was still speaking via dreams even in our days.

When I go through the Bible from Genesis to Revelation, I realized that God is still speaking through dreams.

When you look from the beginning, it was in the dream state that God visited Adam and removed his rib to create the woman.

Examples of some dreams:

- It was in the dream of the night when God visited Abimelech with **warning** concerning Abraham's wife

  Genesis 20 v 3

- It was in the dream of the night when Joseph had a {**promise future dream**} **Genesis 37 v 5**

- It was in the dream of the night when Laban had a **warning dream** concerning Jacob. (Remember, God was protecting Jacob from Laban) **Genesis 31:24**

New Testament:

- It was in the dream when the Angel of God appeared to Joseph with a **protective dream** from King Herod **(Mathew 2 v 13)**

- This is a confirmation dream from Pilate's wife, just to prove Jesus is innocent in this case. She had to send an urgent message to the government that king Pilate

90

respected and obeyed. **(Matthew 27 v 19)**

So, when you go through my testimony, there are different dreams like alarming dreams, confirmation dreams like when He revealed to me when I meet prophet T.B. Joshua and how I would meet him and the place, then the dream being fulfilled physically. The scripture says: **Isaiah 46 v 10:** *Declaring the en*

from the beginning, an *from ancient times the things that are not yet* *one, saying, My counsel shall stan*, *an* *I will* *o all my pleasure:*

It is means what God promise to do, it will come to pass regardless the storm you see in your eyes. The point is He won't deny Himself, delay is not denial.

When God showed me the picture of the prophet in the dream and how I will meet him, it was so unbelievable to me because the situation seemed of no hope. The time I took decision to go and meet him in physically, satan was very furious, situation became worse and worse. Like I said even at the church where the prophet was there, I felt so rejected and developed doubt. I never knew that was the end of my problem.

God made me to understand this scripture that, what he has shown me in the dream from the beginning, He meant it.

When God is with you in the situation; there's no way danger could come without Him alarming you. He promised to go before you and level the mountain.

Some people used to ask me that: Why didn't your God save you before allowing all that you went through to happen? God has the power over everything, including our enemies. He has the power to give life and destroy. He could choose to destroy Herod than to send Joseph to flee to Egypt to hide Jesus. He could have chosen to programme all people on the earth to believe in Him and destroy satan. The point is, He loves us by allowing us to have our own choice. To follow God or to be born again is a choice, not a force that God allows other situations to happen, still knowing that it won't destroy.

At the end of this lesson, permit me to say, dreams are real. What God shows you in spirit, focus on it and forget about what you are seeing in the physical. When you are sick about to die or whatever your situation may look like, then God shows you rising from sickness or that situation, don't make the mistake I did by doubting Him, relax , know that, it will come to pass.

AFTERWORD

I would like to end like this; we need deliverance in many situations especially when we have done everything required spiritually to help ourselves, but problems still refuse to go. For instance, according to my little experience and what I have witnessed from others: Doctors can treat every visible sickness or disease very well, but when it refuses to go, then it's beyond them until God is involved. This is what I mean—we need deliverance in cases like this. It is not only sickness; many prisoners find themselves in prison but don't know how they became prisoners; likewise, prostitutes, divorce cases, e.g., My situations taught me that we shouldn't avoid or condemn these kinds of people and just look at them thinking they have sinned against God. We must listen to them because some of them could be possessed by evil spirits. They just need your prayers or deliverance. If you listen to their cases, you may be a messenger or a channel of rescue.

For instance, I was watching T.D. Jakes TV Show, and

there was a lady who confessed that she had been prostituting from a tender age until she condemned herself that God will never forgive her. Then one lady came to her just to understand why she was doing that; and then she opened up. That's when the lady introduced her to Jesus, and she became born again; her life changed instantly. Now, she is an advisor to those who are still in bondage of the same situation. We have to learn to look beyond what they have done as Christians. I have never known this until I was put through a challenge. Can you imagine if it was not for deliverance, where would I be? I could have been in prison, the baby still in the same situation at the hands of enemies but now my victory is a message to others.

When we are in some situations, these are the weaknesses that most will encounter—doubt, impatience, ignorance of God's messages. All these weaknesses happened to me if you read my testimony very well.

This is the end of my story

Your problems are so different so long as you are in a relationship with Jesus. He is aware; don't give up. Remain blessed. I love you. God is real, but He is not cheap because something would try to eat you first in order for you to eat from it. Imagine our Lord Jesus Christ, He even laid down His life just for us to have victory and before that, it was terrible as people of God were always sacrificing their goats and sheep just to win the battle, but now we are a generation of His grace.

Glory be to God who has given us grace and the gift of righteousness.

Be strengthened!!

Thank you and Be Blessed!!

GLOSSARY

My scriptures: **Isaiah 43 v 1-3**.

This scripture changed my life. Since I caught this scripture in 2011, I don't panic whenever I'm in a situation. Instead, I know that something big is about to happen. This has given me hope that no matter how problems look like, God is with me because He promised that no fire would burn me and no water will overwhelm me. Amen!